Celebrate!

Mexico

Robyn Hardyman

CHELSEA
CLUBHOUSE
An Imprint of Chelsea House Publishers

Copyright © 2009 The Brown Reference Group Ltd.

All rights reserved. No part of this book may be reproduced or utilized in any form or by any means, electronic or mechanical, including photocopying, recording, or by any information storage or retrieval systems, without permission in writing from the publisher. For information contact:

Chelsea Clubhouse
An imprint of Chelsea House
132 West 31st Street
New York, NY 10001

Library of Congress Cataloging-in-Publication Data

Hardyman, Robyn.
  Celebrate Mexico / Robyn Hardyman.
    p. cm. — (Celebrate)
  Includes bibliographical references and index.
  ISBN 978-1-60413-267-0
  1. Mexico—Juvenile literature. I. Title. II. Series.
  F1208.5.H37 2009
  972—dc22
                    2008040131

Chelsea Clubhouse books are available at special discounts when purchased in bulk quantities for businesses, associations, institutions, or sales promotions. Please call our Special Sales Department in New York at (212) 967-8800 or (800) 322-8755.

You can find Chelsea House on the World Wide Web at
http://www.chelseahouse.com

Printed and bound in China

10 9 8 7 6 5 4 3 2 1

This book is printed on acid-free paper.

All links and Web addresses were checked and verified to be correct at the time of publication. Because of the dynamic nature of the Web, some addresses and links may have changed since publication and may no longer be valid.

For The Brown Reference Group Ltd.
Project Editor: Sarah Eason
Designer: Paul Myerscough
Picture Researcher: Maria Joannou
Indexer: Claire Throp
Design Manager: David Poole
Managing Editor: Miranda Smith
Editorial Director: Lindsey Lowe

Consultant Editor
Peter Lewis
Writer and Editor for the American Geographical Society, New York

Author
Robyn Hardyman

Picture Credits
Front Cover: Corbis: Morton Bebe.
Alamy images: Kim Karpeles 8b, Ian Nolan 7t, Mireille Vautier 7b; Bridgeman Art Library: AISA 20l; Corbis: Albright-Knox Art Gallery 22l, Werner Forman 20r, Justin Guariglia 27b, Oliver Weiken/epa 12–13; Dreamstime: Jerl71 11b, 21b, Marcoregalia 15b, Shootalot 28bl; Fotolia: Clarence Alford 27t; Istockphoto: Kelly Cline 3c, James Benet 5l, Robert Ellis 9b, luxxtek 18b, Liza McCorkle 11c, Mafaldita 28–29; Photolibrary: Flirt Collection/Randy Faris 4, Fresh Food Images/Joff Lee 16bl, Imagebroker/Egmont Strigl 8t, JTB Photo 18–19, Robert Harding Travel/Oliviero Olivieri 14bl; Rex Features: CSU Archives/Everett Collection 9t, Tony Larkin 26bl; Shutterstock: Luisa Amare 3t, 15t, Jill Battaglia 17b, Maria Bell 11br, Aura Castro 16–17, Stephen Coburn 29t, Mike Cohen 23t, Evok20 13b, Ken Freeman 23b, Chris Hill 11cr, IntraClique LLC 6b, Goran Kuzmanovski 19b, Ales Liska 5b, Steve Maehl 14r, Igor Marx 26–27, Todd Pierson 29b, Birute Vijeikiene 11tr, Elena Fernandez Zabelguelskaya 6t; Wikipedia: 10br, 12bl, 21t.

Artworks and maps © The Brown Reference Group Ltd.

Contents

Welcome to Mexico

Mexico is the most southerly country in North America. It lies south of the United States. Mexico earns a lot of money from its natural supplies of oil and gas. Despite the country's wealth, there is also poverty in both the countryside and the cities.

United States

Mexico

Mexico

Baja California

Gulf of Mexico

Yucatán Peninsula

Pacific Ocean

Belize

Guatemala

Mexico City

The capital of Mexico is Mexico City. It is one of the biggest cities in the world. Over nineteen million people live there— that's twice the population of New York City. The city center is called the Zócalo. Here you'll find the National Palace, which is the seat of the government.

WEB LINKS ▼▼▼▼▼▼▼▼▼▼▼

To find out more about Mexico City go to:
www.visitmexico.com/wb/Visitmexico/Visi_Ciudad_de_Mexico

Mexico's geography

Mexico shares a land **border** with the United States in the north, and with Guatemala and Belize in the south. The country has two large **peninsulas**: Baja California in the northwest, and the Yucatán Peninsula in the southeast. Mexico's great coastline stretches for 5,798 miles. The country borders the Pacific Ocean to the west, and the Gulf of Mexico and the stunning Caribbean Sea to the east.

MEXICAN FACTS

FULL NAME	United Mexican States
CAPITAL CITY	Mexico City
AREA	761,606 square miles
POPULATION IN 2008	110 million
MAIN LANGUAGES	Spanish, plus more than 50 Mexican Indian languages
MAIN RELIGION	Roman Catholicism
CURRENCY	Peso

Emblem of Mexico

The Mexican coat of arms (left) has been used since 1968. It is based on an old **Aztec** legend—the legend of Tenochtitlán. In the story, the gods told the people that they would build a great city where they saw an eagle eating a snake. That city was Tenochtitlán, which today lies beneath modern Mexico City (see page 7).

Palenque

Palenque (below) is one of the most impressive ancient sites in Mexico. For about 150 years from the beginning of the first century C.E., it was the regional capital of the Mayan **civilization** (see page 6). The stone temples and palaces are decorated with beautiful carvings.

History Highlights

The people who originally lived in Mexico were Mexican Indians. They traveled to Mexico from North America over 20,000 years ago. Since then, Mexico has been home to many great societies.

One of the first civilizations in the Americas was the **Olmecs**. They lived between 1200 and 400 B.C.E. in the eastern coastal lowlands of Mexico, in the area now known as Veracruz. The Olmecs were skilled sculptors. They carved enormous heads, up to nine feet tall, out of rock. The purpose of these sculptures is not known.

The Maya

The Maya civilization lasted from 1000 B.C.E. to 1450 C.E. This advanced society built magnificent stone temples and cities. They created incredible stone artworks, such as the funerary mask (left). These still survive today. The Maya were also mathematicians and astronomers. They developed a calendar with a 365-day year. We still use this calendar today. The Mayan Empire stretched south from the Yucatán Peninsula into Belize, Guatemala, and Honduras.

Jade

The Maya people valued **jade** (a green gemstone) more highly than gold. To them it represented life, fertility, and power. When someone died, a jade bead was placed in their mouth to protect them in the afterlife.

DID YOU KNOW?
The Aztecs decorated many things with gold, which was not considered to be especially precious. Feathers, turquoise, and jade were treasured most highly of all.

The Aztecs

The Aztecs ruled much of Mexico from the fifteenth to the early sixteenth century. Their capital city, Tenochtitlán, was built on an island in the Lake Texcoco, in the Valley of Mexico. They were a warlike but cultured people. They worshipped many gods, and made daily human **sacrifices** to the Sun god. The Aztecs developed a style of picture writing to record events. These writings are called **codices**. They tell us a lot about the Aztec way of life. The codex on the right shows cooking at home.

WEB LINKS
Find out more about the Aztecs at:
www.mexicolore.co.uk/kids/mexkidshome.html

The Spanish arrive

In 1519, a Spanish explorer called Hernán Cortés arrived in Mexico in search of gold and silver. He brought a few hundred armed *conquistadors* with him. These *conquistadors* quickly conquered the Aztecs and took over the country. The Spanish continued to rule Mexico until 1821. They built European-style cities, such as Puebla (left). They also brought their religion, Roman Catholicism, to Mexico. By 1800, they had built more than 12,000 churches there. Life under Spanish rule was difficult for the Mexican people. They had to work hard on the land, or in the silver and gold mines.

Miguel Hidalgo y Costilla

Miguel Hidalgo y Costilla (1753–1811) was a Spanish priest who lived in Dolores, central Mexico. He did not approve of the harsh Spanish rule. In 1810, he encouraged the Mexicans to overthrow their leaders. A rebellion followed, in which Hidalgo was killed. He is regarded as a national hero. This painting shows Hidalgo leading the rebels.

The struggle continues

In 1821, Mexico won its **independence**. In 1876, Porfirio Díaz became **president**. He ruled for over thirty years, and built new roads, railways, and factories, but he did not improve life for the Mexican people. In 1910, the people began a **revolution** against him and won their fight in 1917.

Emiliano Zapata

Emiliano Zapata (1879–1919) was one of the leaders of the Mexican Revolution. He wanted the land to be shared by the people, rather than owned by just a few great landowners. His slogan was "Land and liberty!" Zapata was killed in 1919, but for many Mexicans he remains a national hero.

WEB LINKS ▼▼▼▼▼▼▼▼▼▼▼▼
Find out more about the Mexican Revolution at: www.mexonline.com/revolution.htm

A modern country

In the twentieth century, Mexico developed its industries and became richer. Mexico's oil business is very successful. Other industries include cars, clothing, and beer. The United States is the country's most important trading partner. Three-quarters of Mexico's trade is with the United States. Despite Mexico's growing wealth, most Mexicans are still poor. Every year, many poor Mexicans try to cross the border into the United States to find a job. Over a million of these illegal **immigrants** are arrested.

Fly the Flag

The Mexican flag was chosen by the government after the country won its independence from Spain in 1821.

The Mexican flag is green, white, and red. The green stands for independence, the white for the Roman Catholic religion, and the red for the unity of the people. In the center is Mexico's coat of arms. This shows an eagle with a snake in its beak, perched on a **cactus**. The Festival of the Mexican Flag is celebrated on February 24th each year.

Aztec flag

The Aztecs used symbols to indicate large numbers. The symbol for the number twenty was a flag. The symbol for 100 was therefore five flags, joined by a line.

Huge flags

In 1999, President Ernesto Zedillo ordered giant flags to be erected across the country. The program was known as the *banderas monumentales* (monumental flags). The country's biggest monumental flag is in Monterrey at a public scenic lookout (below). It stands 777 feet above the city and has a pole 330 feet high. The flag is 164 x 94 feet in size. This place is a very attractive landmark for tourists as well as for locals.

The golden eagle at the center of the flag is the national animal of Mexico.

WEB LINKS ▼▼▼▼▼
Find out more about the Mexican flag at: www.mexican-flag.org

Dahlia
The dahlia is the national flower of Mexico. Dahlias were first cultivated by the Aztecs, and still grow in large numbers in the mountains.

🇲🇽 Try this!
Make a Mexico poster

- Using this book, the Internet, and other reference sources, compile a list of Mexican things that you would like to display on your poster. These could be pictures of Mexican foods, different landscapes, towns, buildings, key people from Mexican history, Native Mexican peoples, works of art from past civilizations such as the Aztecs, and Spanish words.

- Research and gather images of the objects online, and in magazines. Cut out the images, and arrange them on a large piece of cardboard.

- Write "MEXICO" across the top of your poster, and glue a large Mexican flag in one corner. You could put a map in the other corner.

- Glue all the pictures onto the cardboard, and display your "Mexico" poster on your bedroom wall.

Hymn to Mexico

Mexico's national anthem was chosen in 1854, thirty-three years after independence in 1821. It has no official name, but it is sometimes called "Mexicanos, al grito de guerra," which means "Mexicans, at the cry of war."

The lyrics of the anthem were written in 1853 by a poet named Francisco González Bocanegra (1824–61). The lyrics refer to Mexico's victories in battle, and its struggle for independence. The words encourage feelings of national unity and celebrate Mexico's identity. The poem has ten verses and a chorus, but only four verses are sung as the anthem. The anthem's music and some of the words are shown below and right.

Chorus

Mexicans, at the cry of war,
Make ready your sword and horse,
Let the core of your land resound,
To the sonorous roar of the cannon.

Verse 1

Fatherland! Be crowned with the olive branch
Of peace by the divine archangel.
For in heaven your eternal destiny
Was written by the finger of God.
But if a foreign enemy dares
To **profane** your land with his foot,
Remember, dear fatherland, that heaven
Has given you a soldier in each son.

WEB LINKS ▼▼▼▼▼▼▼
To listen to the Mexican national anthem go to:
www.national-anthems.net/MX

Sporting pride

Supporters of Mexico's soccer team sing the **national anthem** before the 2006 World Cup match between Argentina and Mexico in Germany.

DID YOU KNOW?

A competition was held to find the music for the national anthem. The winner was a Spanish composer called Jaime Nunó (1824–1908). He was the leader of several military bands.

Learning lyrics

The Mexican federal government has been known to fine people who do not perform their national anthem correctly. When a performer forgot some of the lyrics at a soccer match in the city of Guadalajara, she was fined forty U.S. dollars by the Interior Ministry.

Song and dance

Mexicans have a long tradition of folk singing and dancing. Traditional folk dancers wear beautiful dresses with full skirts, such as the one shown right. The skirt has many layers and is often edged with lace or embroidered at the bottom. The upper part of the dress is loose fitting and has wide sleeves.

Regions of Mexico

Mexico has three quite different regions. The north is very dry, and few people live there. The central area, which is mainly highland, is the most heavily populated place. The south and the Yucatán Peninsula are hot and steamy, with scattered towns.

Dry desert

Almost half of Mexico is desert. Spiky plants called cacti grow well here. In some years, no rain falls at all. Farming is only possible near rivers, and places watered by underground springs.

Mexico has three chains of mountains: the western, eastern, and southern Sierra Madre. They enclose a large highland region called the Mexican **Plateau**. The western Sierra Madre is remote and rugged. It is home to the Copper Canyon (below), which is made up of five connected canyons. It is even wider and deeper than the Grand Canyon in the United States.

Yucatán Peninsula

The Yucatán Peninsula does not have many towns. It does, however, have beautiful **rain forests** that are home to many unusual animals and plants. It also has Mexico's most famous beach resort, Cancún. The miles of sandy beaches found here are popular with both Mexican and foreign tourists.

DID YOU KNOW?

Mexico is so dry and mountainous that only 12 percent of the land can be used for farming. Despite this, much of the working population still make their living from the land. They grow crops and raise animals.

MEXICAN FACTS

LONGEST RIVER	Rio Bravo del Norte (Rio Grande in the U.S.) 1,880 miles
HIGHEST MOUNTAIN	Pico de Orizaba 18,490 feet
LARGEST CITIES	Mexico City, Ecatepec, Guadalajara

Natural disasters

Mexico has many volcanoes, including Popocatépetl (below), and Iztaccíhuatl near Mexico City. The country also suffers from earthquakes, and violent hurricanes. **In 1985, a severe earthquake caused terrible damage to Mexico City. More than 6,000 people were killed.**

What's Cooking?

Mealtimes are an important part of family life in Mexico. The food is a mixture of Spanish and Indian cooking. Many people like to eat spicy foods. Eating out at restaurants is popular in the cities.

Most people in Mexico eat their main meal in the middle of the day. This is called *comida*. It consists of three courses: a starter, a main course, and pudding. After *comida* people often take a **siesta** (a rest).

Tortillas, beans, and chocolate chili

The country's main ingredient is corn, or maize. This is made into flat pancakes called *tortillas*. These can be rolled around fillings or toasted and topped with cheese. Meat, beans, and chili peppers are used in many dishes. Sometimes chocolate is added to meals, such as the beef chili shown left.

Tasty *tacos*

Tacos are very versatile because they can be filled with any meat, fish, or vegetable mixture. They are usually eaten with one's hands, and taste great with *salsa*.

DID YOU KNOW?

Mexico's national alcoholic drink is *tequila*. This strong spirit is made from a cactus plant called "blue agave." Worms are sometimes added to *tequila* bottles—when all the drink has been finished, some brave people eat the worm!

What's on the menu?

A typical *comida* starts with soup, and is followed by rice.

Sopa de Fideos con Acelgas
Mexican noodle soup with chard

Arroz Blanco con Verduras
White rice with vegetables

Pollo en Salsa de Almendras
Chicken in almond sauce

Frijoles de Olla
Beans in their own broth

Flan de Coco
Coconut flan

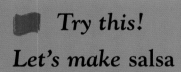 ## Try this!
Let's make salsa

Ingredients:
1 small onion
2 mild chili peppers
4 large ripe tomatoes
juice of 1 lime
salt
handful of coriander
    leaves

Ask an adult to help you finely chop the onions, chili peppers, and tomatoes and put them in a bowl. Add the lime juice and a pinch of salt. Mix well. Chop the coriander leaves, and add them to the bowl. Allow the salsa to stand until you are ready to enjoy as a dip.

How Do I Say...?

Mexico was once ruled by Spain, so most Mexican people speak Spanish. Many people also speak the languages of the native Mexican Indians.

Although Spanish is the official language in Mexico, more than fifty different native Indian languages are also spoken. The use of these languages has diminished since the Spanish first arrived in the fifteenth century. Now only 6 percent of the population speak a native language.

Warning sign
This school crossing sign means "slowly." "Despacio" is said "des-pah'-che-o."

Words and phrases

English	Spanish	How to say it
hello	hola	o-la
goodbye	adios	add-ios
yes	sí	see
no	no	no
good morning	buenos días	bway-nos dee-as
my name is...	me llamo	meh yah-mo
please	por favor	paw-fa-vaw
thank you	gracias	grah-see-ahs

WEB LINKS
Listen to some useful Spanish phrases spoken at:
www.relax-in-spain.com/basic-holiday-spanish.html

Native languages

Many of the ancient Indian languages have died out, but some are still spoken today. The language of the Aztecs, Náhuatl, is still spoken widely among native Indians. The Tarahumara Indians live in the region of the Copper Canyon in northern Mexico. They have their own language, Raramuri. Every summer, members of the seven main native Mexican Indian groups gather in the state of Oaxaca for a celebration called Guelaguetza. They parade through the streets in traditional costumes, display their local handicrafts, and perform traditional songs and dances.

DID YOU KNOW?
Today, there are very few pure native Indians left in Mexico. Most Mexicans are *mestizo*, which means they are descendants of native Indians and Spanish settlers. Only about 19 percent of the people can claim to be pure native Indians.

Some Mexican sayings

"Camarón que se duerme se lo lleva la corriente"
meaning: "A shrimp that sleeps gets carried away by the tide."

"Más vale un pájaro en mano que ver un ciento volar" meaning: "A bird in your hand is worth more than a hundred in flight."

"Hay más tiempo que vida" meaning: "There is more time than life."

Stories and Legends

Mexico's rich history of good writing dates back to the times before Spanish conquerors took over the country.

The Aztecs believed that the gods lived above the Earth in thirteen layers of heaven. The most powerful gods lived in the top layer. The most important god was Huitzilopochtli, the Sun god and god of war. The water goddess was Chalchihuitlicue. She was married to the god of rain, Tlaloc. The god of the wind was Quetzalcoatl. He was also the god of learning. The Aztecs made masks of the gods (right), decorated with the precious stone turquoise.

Skin of a god

In Aztec mythology, Xipe Totec was a god of agriculture and the seasons. An Aztec legend tells of how he peeled off his own skin in order to feed the world. In honor of Xipe Totec, slaves were sacrificed by having their skin peeled off too. The skin of the dead slave was then worn by a priest during the fertility rituals that followed the sacrifice.

Carlos Fuentes

Carlos Fuentes (born 1928) is a famous Mexican writer, and one of the best known living writers in the Spanish speaking world. He writes novels, plays, and essays. He often writes about the history and identity of Mexico and its people.

Tlaloc

The Aztecs believed that Tlaloc, god of rain, made people sick by striking them down with a lightning bolt! Human sacrifices were often made in his honor, usually using children. This is an image of Tlaloc from a codex called Rios.

Ancient poetry

The ancient peoples of Mexico wrote poetry and holy writings. In the fifteenth century, the king of the city of Texcoco wrote poems that were sung at his court. One of the king's poems is shown to the right.

Just like a painting,
We will be dimmed.
Just like a flower,
We shall wither.
Think of this,
Eagle and jaguar knights,
Though you were carved in jade,
Though you were made of gold,
You too will go there,
To the land of the fleshless.
All things must vanish,
None may remain.

Mexico's volcanoes

Popocatépetl and Iztaccíhuatl are two volcanoes. In Aztec legend, the mountains were created by Popo, a fierce warrior. Popo was in love with Ixta, the daughter of the emperor. While Popo was away fighting, Ixta was tricked into thinking he was dead, and she died of grief. On his return, Popo laid her body on top of Iztaccíhuatl and stood guard over her, holding a smoking torch. The lovers then turned to stone.

DID YOU KNOW?
Iztaccíhuatl (below) has four peaks, which resemble the head, chest, knees, and feet of a sleeping woman.

Art and Culture

Mexican arts reflect the rich mixture of traditions and cultures found in the country. Much Mexican art is linked to people's religious beliefs. Art objects are often practical as well as beautiful. For example, people weave striking cloth and make attractive pots and jewelry.

Diego Rivera and Frida Kahlo

Diego Rivera and Frida Kahlo were Mexican artists who were married to each other. Diego Rivera (1886–1957) painted public murals for everyone to enjoy. His favorite subjects were everyday and traditional Mexican scenes. Frida Kahlo (1907–54) was ill throughout her life. Her own suffering influenced her art. She painted many self-portraits (left) and scenes of Mexican life.

Sun city

Teotihuacán was one of the greatest ancient Mexican cities. By about 550 C.E., around 150,000 people lived there. The Pyramid of the Sun, left, was built around 150 C.E. It is one of the biggest buildings in the world. It is over 200 feet high, and is made of clay faced with blocks of stone. A temple originally stood on the top.

Tired feet

People all over Mexico wear sandals called *huaraches* that are made of rubber from used car tires!

Textiles

Mexican women often make clothes for themselves using traditional techniques. In rural areas, they may dye the threads, and then weave them into bright textiles. For thousands of years, people have been using a backstrap loom for weaving. One end is fixed to a tree or pillar, the other is tied around the weaver's body. Each region of the country has its own dress style and weaving patterns.

Pottery

Mexico is well known for its clay pottery. Some of the techniques used today were first introduced by the Aztecs hundreds of years ago. Pots may be used to store grain and water, and for cooking. Colorful tiles are used to decorate homes, inside and outside.

Make Your Own Mexican Armadillo

Make this clay armadillo to give to a friend. Or keep it yourself as a reminder of all the wonderful facts you have learned about Mexico.

You will need:
- modeling clay from a craft shop
- sponge
- toothpicks
- poster paints
- paintbrush
- scissors

1 To make the body, roll out a ball of clay about the size of a tennis ball. Press your thumb into the middle of it, and hollow it out by squeezing the clay between your fingers and thumb. Flatten the open edge by tapping it gently on a flat surface.

2 Make a neck hole at the front of the body shape. Pull up the edges of the neck to make a collar, as shown left.

Armored animal

The word "armadillo" means "man in armor," in Spanish. The animal of this name is certainly very well protected by its tough covering. It has long claws and strong legs, which it uses to dig for ants. It lives in Mexico, and Central and South America.

3 To make the head, roll out a small ball of clay. Press one end into a triangle shape, and the other into a sausage shape. Pinch up the ears, as shown above.

4 Roll out four smaller balls of clay for the feet, and a short sausage shape for the tail. Moisten the surfaces using the sponge and water, then stick the feet and tail to the body. Blend the clay edges together, so that you cannot see the seams.

5 Hold the head in the neck hole. Carefully push a toothpick through one side of the hole and out the other side as shown right. Leave it to dry.

6 When the clay has hardened, remove the toothpick and the head from the body. Paint the armadillo in bright colors.

7 Reattach the head by pushing the toothpick back through its old holes. Trim off the ends of the toothpick with a pair of scissors. Find a good place to display your new friend.

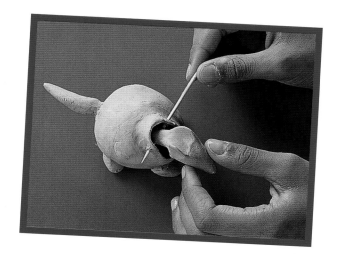

Sports and Leisure

The people of Mexico love sports. They watch and play soccer, basketball, and volleyball, as well as other sports native to their country.

Mexicans adore *futbol*, or soccer. The game is played in every village and town, and people everywhere support their **league** sides and the national team. The two most popular teams are América, nicknamed "The Eagles," and Guadaljara nicknamed "The Goats." They play each other at the enormous Aztec Stadium in Mexico City. Some supporters of the Mexico national team wear elaborate headgear like the one shown right.

Wrestling

The second most popular spectator sport is masked wrestling, or *lucha libre*. The masks are used to conceal the identity of the wrestlers. This sport is faster and more aggressive than traditional wrestling. There may even be more than two wrestlers in the ring at the same time.

Bullfighting

On Sunday afternoons, Mexicans go to the bullring to watch the bullfights. A dashing **matador** in a colorful costume tests his skill against the massive bull. The matador swirls his cape around to bait the bull, then tries to kill it with a sword between the shoulders. It is a tense and exciting, but also rather brutal, spectacle.

A day of rest

On Sundays, many Mexicans put on their best clothes and go to church. Afterward they might go out for a meal with family and friends, or for a picnic on the beach or in the park. People enjoy listening to traditional folk groups playing in cafés and plazas.

DID YOU KNOW?
Charrería is a series of Mexican equestrian events. The main event is the *charreada,* a type of rodeo.

WEB LINKS
Find out more about bullfighting at:
www.aboutmexico.net/mexico/bullfighting.asp

Festivals and Holidays

Festivals are an important part of life in Mexico. Some are celebrated throughout the country, others are more local. Craftspeople sell special decorations for people to hang from their homes and churches during these happy occasions.

Independence day

On September 16th, Mexicans celebrate their independence from Spain. Helmets and trumpets in red, white, and green are seen everywhere. People dress in costume to parade and dance in the streets, traditional foods are sold, and fireworks are set off. On May 5th, there is a festival called Cinco de Mayo, which celebrates the day in 1862 when Mexico defeated the French army. The battle is reenacted, and everyone takes to the streets to celebrate.

Day of the Dead

The Day of the Dead is Mexico's most famous festival. It is the time when people remember members of their family who have died. They take presents to the graves of their relatives. They then prepare a feast for the spirits of the dead. They give each other sweets in the shape of skulls (left).

Puppets and *piñatas*

Giant puppets called *mojigangas* are paraded down the streets during carnivals and festivals. At feasts, birthdays, and Christmas, children celebrate with a *piñata*, a paper container filled with sweets and small toys. They take turns swinging a stick at the *piñata* in an attempt to smash it and free the contents.

The Virgin of Guadalupe

On December 12th, Mexicans celebrate the feast of the Virgin of Guadalupe, the patron saint of Mexico. The event remembers the day that the Virgin Mary appeared to a poor boy called Juan Diego in Guadalupe. Children dress in traditional Mexican costume and go to church.

Masks and dancing

Each festival has its own dance. The Tiger Dance is part of the Day of the Dead festival. Dancers, wearing masks, pretend to be tigers damaging the crops. Other dancers chase them away.

Glossary

Aztecs Mexican people that existed from 1427–1521

astronomers people who study the stars and planets

border frontier between two countries

cactus spiny-leaved plant

civilizations organized societies

codices ancient documents

conquistadors Spanish soldiers who conquered Mexico, Central America, and Peru in the sixteenth century

federal area controlled by a central, rather than a local, government

hurricanes violent storms with strong winds and heavy rain

immigrants people who move to another country to live there permanently

independence freedom from control

jade green precious stone valued by the Maya

league group of teams that compete against one another

matador bullfighter

Mayan describes a civilization that existed in Central America from around 1000 B.C.E. to 1450 C.E.

mestizo person of mixed European (usually Spanish) and native heritage

murals paintings on a wall

national anthem song of a country

Olmecs people from a civilization in the Americas that existed from 1200 to 400 B.C.E.

patron saint saint who is believed to protect a particular place or activity

peninsulas narrow strips of land that reach out into the sea

plateau area of high, flat land

president person who runs a country, elected by the people

profane to treat with disrespect

rain forests densely forested areas that receive heavy rainfall and are rich with plant and animal life

rebellion organized opposition

revolution violent uprising by the people to overthrow the government

sacrifices ceremonies in which a creature is killed and offered to the gods

self-portraits portraits an artist makes of himself or herself

siesta a rest, or nap, usually taken in the early afternoon

tequila Mexican spirit made from agave

turquoise greenish-blue stone

Find Out More

Books

Campbell-Hinshaw, Kelly. *Art Across the Ages: Ancient Mexico*. Chronicle Books, 2007

Goulding, Sylvia. *Festive Foods: Mexico*. Chelsea Clubhouse, 2008

Guzman, Lila and Rick. *Diego Rivera: Artist of Mexico*. Enslow Elementary, 2006

Hoyt-Goldsmith, Diane. *Cinco De Mayo: Celebrating the Traditions of Mexico*. Holiday House, 2008

Stein, R. Conrad. *Enchantment of the World: Mexico*. Children's Press, 2006

Turck, Mary C. *Mexico & Central America: A Fiesta of Cultures, Crafts, and Activities for Ages 8-12*. Chicago Review Press, 2004

Zronik, John Paul. *Hernando Cortés: Spanish Invader of Mexico*. Crabtree Publishing, 2006

Web sites

www.visitmexico.com
This is a great Web site for information on all aspects of life in Mexico.

www.mexonline.com/states.htm
Check out the useful guides to Mexico's cities and states at this Web site.

www.aboutmexico.net
This Web site is particularly good on places to visit in Mexico.

www.nationalmuseumofmexicanart.org
Discover more about the varied arts of Mexico at the Web site of this museum dedicated to the subject.

www.texmextogo.com/recipes.htm
Find recipes and information about Mexican food at this helpful Web site.

Index